Karma and *Jñāna* in Śaṅkara's Advaita Vedānta

Interfaith Treasures Uncovered

Under this Series, the Publishers endeavor to focus on Comparative Studies pertaining to Christian Faith & Living in the central matrix and Hinduism, Buddhism, Sikhism, Islam, Judaism, etc., on the peripheral. The Studies shall cover topics like Literature & Poetry, Indigenous Philosophizing, Ethical response towards Agriculture, Health & Healing, Science & Technology, Ecofeminist Theology, Sociological approach towards Human Rights, Law & Politics, Arts, History of Ideas, Ancient Civilizations, Cultural Contiguity, Religious Cosmologies & Mysticism, Footsteps of famous Theologians, World Peace & Harmony, Global Capitalism, Network Marketing, Cybertheology, Population & Demographics, Epigraphic Studies, Contextualized Education, and many others. We welcome a Mss. on any topic/s mentioned, whether they are original works, scholarly monographs, collections of conference papers, revised dissertations, or translations of historical documents. Through the Series, we are striving to put forward published works that may help Institutions, Academic Bodies, Researchers, Scholars and the World at large in furthering their respective knowledge and understanding on the concerned subject. We welcome your comments on our efforts and further suggestions on how we can foster the upcoming books on parallel interfaces between and among Christianity and other religions.

Interfaith Treasures Uncovered - 18

Karma and *Jñāna* in Śaṅkara's Advaita Vedānta

A Theological and Philosophical Interpretation

Rodinmawia Ralte

CWI

Christian World Imprints

First Published in 2019 by

Christian World Imprints
Christian Publishing & Books from India
H-12 Bali Nagar, **New Delhi-110015**
info@christianworldimprints.com
www.ChristianWorldImprints.com
Phone: +91 11 25465925

ISBN: 978-93-5148-347-2

Printed in India.

Contents

Preface

This booklet is the product of my sincere research into the Advaita Vedānta of Śaṅkara and I am happy that it comes out in a book form for the public readers especially for those who are interested in Śaṅkara's theology/philosophy. Though the book is small, I feel that the content is big, in the sense that I have put my bold argument that for Śaṅkara, *karma yoga* is important or rather indispensable for self-realization which many scholars and students of Śaṅkara may want to oppose it strongly. That is why this booklet is interesting and important. I wish that this booklet will throw some lights into the study of Śaṅkara and provoke scholars in this area to study more and probe deeper into the matter to bring out more hidden things in Śaṅkara's Advaita Vedānta.

I thank my good friend, Shri Sudhanshu and the Christian World Imprints for their interest to publish this material. May God, the Ultimate Reality, bless this book for all the readers.

Rodinmawia Ralte
Hnahthial, Mizoram

Introduction

Of all Indian thinkers there may be no one who is more misunderstood than Śaṅkara, although he has shown no ambiguity throughout his writings. Surendranath Bhattacharya's comment is well taken: "He combined profundity of thought with clarity of expression – a combination rare in philosophical writings."[1] Śaṅkara, the medieval spiritual and intellectual giant, uses simple language but writes profound theological and philosophical piece but is still misinterpreted and misunderstood by many scholars. Professor R. De Smet identifies three basic reasons as to why Śaṅkara is misunderstood and misrepresented by scholars, such as, unsystematic presentation of his works (most of his works are commentary on Scriptures), inadequate vocabulary (he uses Sāṃkhya language and does not create many new terms to express his thought) and influence of spurious works (so many works that bear the name of Śaṅkara which influence some of his later followers and interpreters, are not genuine Śaṅkara's writings).[2]

---

[1] Surendranath Bhattacharya, "The Philosophy of Śaṅkara", in *The Cultural Heritage of India*, Vol. III, edited by Haridas Bhattacharyya, (Calcutta: Ramakrishna Mission Institute of Culture, 1993), p. 237.

[2] R. De Smet, "Śaṅkara's Non-dualism (Advaita-Vāda)", in *Religious Hinduism*, edited by R. De Smet and J. Neuner, Fourth Revised Edition, (Mumbai: St. Pauls, 1997), p. 81.

This research work is a daring attempt to rectify one of such erroneous interpretations of Śaṅkara.

1. THE PROBLEM

The research problem is to investigate and establish the assumed reality of the integral relationship between *Karma yoga* and *Jñāna yoga* for Self-realization as presented by Śaṅkarāchārya in his theological/philosophical writings.

There is an elusive notion and seeming contradiction in Śaṅkara's method for Self-realization. In the introduction to his *Bhagavad Gitā Bhāṣya*, Sankara points out that the Lord gave twofold Vedic religion – the religion of work (*Pravṛitti-Dharma*) and the religion of renunciation of work (*Nivṛitti-Dharma*) for the people. He writes, "It is the twofold Vedic Religion of Works and Renunciation that maintain order in the universe."[3] It follows that Śaṅkara recognizes two ways, such as, *Karma Yoga* and *Jñāna Yoga* for Self-realization. However, throughout his Bhagavad Gita *Bhāṣya*, Śankara maintains that liberation is attained by knowledge alone and not by Work.[4] But at the same time he says that both *Karma yoga* and *Jñāna yoga* lead to the same goal, that is, liberation.[5] Śaṅkara upholds the Lord as telling Arjuna, when the later inquired as to which one of these two is better and which one he will follow, that *Karma Yoga* is better and that he (Arjuna) should resort to following this path.[6] So, it is apparent that Śaṅkara accepts *Karma yoga* and even advises Arjuna to follow as a method for Self-realization. In this regard, Chatterjee and Datta also remark: "Śaṅkara attaches great importance to disinterested work... such work is necessary for self purification (*ātma-śuddhi*)... In his own life of intense social service Śaṅkara

[3] Śankarāchārya, *Bhagavad Gītā Commentary*, translated by A. Mahadeva Shastri, (Mysore: Government Oriental Library, 1901), p. 2.

[4] *B.G.B.* II:10; III:17; XVIII:50.

[5] *B.G.B.* V:2; V:4.

[6] *B.G.B.* V:2.

follows this ideal."[7] Thus, it is apparent that Śaṅkara contradicts himself by saying Knowledge (*jñāna*) alone liberates and at the same time maintaining that Work (*karma*) is also leading to liberation and in fact better to tread for people like Arjuna.

Furthermore, in his *Brahma Sūtra Bhāṣya* (*B.S.*), Śaṅkara by way of refuting Mīmāmsākas who had preferential option for Vedic rituals (*Karma Yoga*), consistently maintains that Knowledge is the only way for Self-realization and that Vedic sacrifices has no ontological value insofar as liberation of the bonded *jīva* and the attainment of Brahman is concerned. Furthermore, Śaṅkara negates the necessity of religious rites of the Vedas as the prerequisite for attaining Brahman because he feels that deliberation on Upaniṣads is enough.[8] Religious rite and the study of the Upaniṣads have no sequence because rites have secular prosperity as their result whereas the knowledge of Brahman has emancipation as its result.[9] Śaṅkara even says, "The Vedas reveal that the *Agnihotra* sacrifices, etc., which are the means for the achievement of higher things have evanescent results."[10] He further argues that as the Self is not the sphere of any action, the Self can have no action occurring on Itself, so action cannot purified the Self.[11] More emphatically he notes: "Liberation is a state of identity with Brahman and hence it is not to be achieved through purification (by action) … apart from knowledge alone there cannot be a lightest touch of action here."[12]

In the same vein Śaṅkara also writes, "The results of actions are the production, acquisition, transformation and purification of something. They produce no other results. All actions with

---

[7] Satischandra Chatterjee and Dhirendramohan Datta, *An Introduction to Indian Philosophy,* Calcutta: University of Calcutta, 2004, p. 410.

[8] Śaṅkarāchārya, *Brahmasūtras Bhāṣya,* (*B.S*) 1.1.1, translated by Swami Gambhirananda, Calcutta: Advaita Aśrama, 1993, p. 7.

[9] *B.S.* 1.1.1; 1.1.4, in *Ibid*., pp. 8 & 26.

[10] *B.S.* 1.1.1. in *Ibid*., p. 9.

[11] *B.S.* 1.1.4, in *Ibid*., p. 33.

[12] *B.S.* 1.1.4, in *Ibid*., p. 34.

their accessories should, therefore, be given up,"[13] indicating that knowledge not works is the way for Self-realization. However, on the other hand Śaṅkara does not fail to recognize the importance of *Karma*, he says that without performance of actions, the saving knowledge cannot dawn at all.[14] He also says that sacrifices which are the duties of the respective stages of life are all but means for the emergence of knowledge[15] – thereby suggesting the integral and inseparable relationship between work and knowledge for Self-realization.

Therefore, in the mind of the researcher, there are a number of questions such as: What is the place of *Karma Yoga* in Saṅkara's theology of salvation? What is the importance of *work*? How *karma* and *jñāna* are related, if at all they are related? Is the conjunction of these two was what Śaṅkara prescribed? Or Is there no relationship between these two at all? Did Śaṅkara, by rejecting another two traditional methods of salvation, such as *Karma* and *Bhakti*, prescribe *Jñāna yoga* alone as the mean for Self-realization as many people have projected him as doing it? Or, what is (if any) the integral relationship between *Karma yoga* (works without attachment) and *Jñāna* (renunciation of work, i.e., realized knowledge) for the attainment of liberation? These and the likes are some of the questions which are discussed in this book.

2. THE METHOD

Religion, be it taken wholly or partly is too complex to approach by using one method alone. So, the intricacy of religion demands a poly-methodic approach in order to arrive at the reality of any religious teaching. This is applicable to the study of Śaṅkara and his theology/philosophy as well. *First*, to understand Śaṅkara correctly we need to consider some of the misinterpretations of

---

[13] *Upadeśasāhasrī*, Chapter XVII: 50, in Swami Jagadananda (Trans.), *Upadeśasāhasrī of Śaṅkaracharya*, (Madras: Sri Ramakrishna Math, 1949), p. 206.

[14] *B.S.* III.4.26.

[15] *B.S.* III.4.27.

Śaṅkara within and without his own tradition by identifying the authentic works of Śaṅkara and work on them for the reason that such misinterpretations happened because many interpreters worked on the un-genuine Śaṅkara's writings that produced a distorted picture of his philosophy. *Secondly*, he employs a particular type of hermeneutical principle in his commentaries, that is, the 'theory of implication' (*lakṣaṇā*) method. He uses the words of ordinary language according to some definite meaning which he is perfectly aware. He means their express meaning (*mukhyārtha*) when the things he speaks of belong to the phenomenal realm. He means their implied meaning (*laksyārtha*) when he deals with things which transcend phenomenal realm.[16] Again, Śaṅkara introduces the distinction of a common-sense view (*vyāvahārika*) and philosophic view (*pāramārthika*) to explain the scriptures.[17] So, it is necessary to employ his own hermeneutical principles to study his doctrine. *Thirdly*, Śaṅkara, throughout his commentaries, makes an attempt to interpret scripture by scripture, so it is indispensable in our approach also to interpret Śaṅkara by Śaṅkara in order to arrive at the inwardness and the inner meanings of his teachings. (*A brief discussion on Sankara's theological method is given in Chapter 2*).

So, in this study a *historical-analytical* method coupled with what has been discussed above is employed where authentic sources will be identified and an analysis will be done from them. Here, a study is done from the authentic works of Śaṅkara, for which his Bhagavad Gītā *Bhāṣya* is found to be the most important source, of course, without overlooking his other works such as *Brahma Sūtra Bhāṣya*, commentaries on nine Upaniṣads and the independent treaties – *Upadeśa-Sāhasrī*. From these sources, careful and systematic analysis is made, allowing Śaṅkara to

---

[16] K.P. Aleaz, *The Relevance of Relation in* Śaṅkara*'s Advaita Vedānta*, (Delhi: Kant Publications, 1996), pp. 25-26.

[17] Surendranath Dasgupta, *A History of Indian Philosophy*, Vol. II, (Delhi: Motilal Banarsidass, 1975 – first published in 1922 by Cambridge University Press), p. 2.

speak for himself to arrive at the reality of his teaching on *Karma marga* and *Jñāna marga* for Self-realization.

We started our discussion with the highlights of Śaṅkara's life and his teaching in chapter one. Chapter two deals with his theological method where we make an attempt to rectify some of the misinterpretations of Śaṅkara and moved on to the discussion on his interaction with Mīmāmsā in chapter three. The fourth chapter deals with his interpretation of *Karma Yoga* in Bhagavad Gītā and the relationship between Work and Knowledge according to Śaṅkara's advaita Vedānta is discussed in chapter five.

Chapter 1

The Life and Thought of Śaṅkara: An Overview

Śaṅkara is undoubtedly the most influential thinker and religious genius in medieval and modern India. He is endowed with supernatural gift: "metaphysical genius, faultless acumen, dexterous logic, incomparable eruption and unshakeable faith."[1] His contribution towards the resurgence of Hinduism is so great that it is no wonder to be described as 'the greatest intellect of the world' and 'the most towering personality of Hinduism in its renaissance period.'[2] There is confusion, however, concerning his life and his teachings as a number of contradictory accounts have come down to us but conversely this only serves as an indicator of his greatness. This chapter presents a brief account of the life and teachings of Śaṅkara.

[1] R. De Smet, "Śaṅkara's Non-dualism (Advaita-Vāda)", in *Religious Hinduism*, edited by R. De Smet and J. Neuner, Fourth Revised Edition, (Mumbai: St. Pauls, 1997), p. 81.

[2] W.S. Urquhart, *The Vedanta and Modern Thought*, (London: Oxford University Press, 1928), p. 51.

1. The Life of Śaṅkara

There is hardly any agreement among scholars concerning the facts of Śaṅkara's life though plenteous traditions are with us narrating contradictory stories about him. C.N. Krishnaswami Aiyer may be right when he says, "Few of the facts of his life can be narrated with certainty, not even the time and the place of his birth."[3] It is beyond the purview of this book to go deep into the various arguments concerning his life and attempt to deduce the most obvious one, but it brings a brief account of his life which is more or less accepted by most of the scholars and specialists in the study of Śaṅkara's life and thought with a reservation that what has been reproduced here is also subject to disagreement.

1.1. Sources

There are ten *Śaṅkara-Vijaya* (Biographies of Śaṅkara) identified by T.S. Narayana Sastri in his book *The Age of Saṅkara*.[4] These *Śaṅkara-Vijayas* are accepted generally as the source book for the life of Śaṅkara. However, out of these ten,[5] only five are printed and even most of them are very rare to find. The five printed *Śaṅkara-Vijaya* are - *Śaṅkara-Vijaya* of Aanntānandagiri, *Śaṅkara-Vijaya* of Govindanātha, *Śaṅkara-Vijaya* of Villisahāyakavi, *Śaṅkara-Vijaya* of Chitvilāsa, *Śaṅkara-Vijaya* of Mādhava.[6]

---

[3] C.N. Krishnaswami Aiyer, "Life and Time of Saṅkara", in *Three Great Acharyas: Śaṅkara, Ramanuja, Madhwa: Critical Sketches of their Life and Times, an Expositions of their Philosophical System*, (Madras: G.A. Natesan & Co., Publishers, No year of publication), p. 1.

[4] T.S. Narayana Aier, *The Age of Saṅkara*, (Madras: B.G. Paul & Co., 1971; first published in 1916), p. 32.

[5] The ten *Śaṅkara-Vijaya* are – (1) *Śaṅkara-Vijaya* of Sri Chitsukhāchārya, one of the direct disciple of and co-student of Śaṅkara, (2) *Śaṅkara-Vijaya* Ānandagiri, (3) *Śaṅkara-Vijaya* of Vidyā Śaṅkara or Śaṅkarānanda, (4) *Śaṅkara-Vijaya* of Govindanātha, (5) *Śaṅkara-Vijaya* of Chūdāmani Dikshita, (6) *Śaṅkara-Vijaya* of Aanntānandagiri, (7) *Śaṅkara-Vijaya* of Villisahāyakavi, (8) *Śaṅkara-Vijaya* of Sadānanda, (9) *Śaṅkara-Vijaya* of Chitvilāsa, (10) *Śaṅkara-Vijaya* of Mādhava. In *Ibid*., pp. 32-33.

[6] Cf. Swami Tapasyananda in the "Introduction" to Madhva-Vidyaranya, *Śaṅkara-Dig-Vijaya: The Traditional Life of Sri Śaṅkarācharya*, translated by Swami

Those unprinted manuscripts are not available to us any longer. According to Narayana Sastri there are some other sources preserved by various Advaitic Maths which talk about Śaṅkara,[7] but scholars are not interested in them as their authenticity cannot be proved. It is to be noted here that most of the books and materials concerning the life of Śaṅkara are based on the above five *Śaṅkara-Vijaya*, of which the latest one, considered to be written by the great Mādhavācharya, is the most popular and widely circulated. However, this account is not a historical piece but more of philosophical treatise full of legends in need of filtering to get the historical facts of Śaṅkara's life.

1.2. A Brief Sketch of His Life

There is no consensus among scholars regarding the time of Śaṅkara's birth and death except that he is considered to have a short life. In the midst of several suggestions, the most accepted date is 788-820 A.D. but this is also not without disputation. Swami Tapasyananda, in his Introduction to *Śaṅkara-Dig-Vijaya*, after discussing at length the possible date of Śaṅkara, concludes in a dejective mood thus, "Vastly varied are the views about Śaṅkara's date, ranging from 509 B.C. to 788 A.D., i.e., more than a millennium and a half."[8] This indicates that we do not know for sure the exact date of Śaṅkara's birth and death. He was born probably at a small village known by the name Kaladi in Kerela. His father Śivaguru and mother Aryamba were endowed with all good things of life but a son. The traditions maintain that the couple went to a Śiva Temple for *bhajanam* – worship and prayer. While spending their time in the temple, Lord Śiva in the form of an old man appeared in the dream of Śivaguru to fulfill his heart-felt desire – a baby boy. He asked him to choose between several dull-witted sons who would live long or a single brilliant

---

Tapasyananda, (Madras: Sri Ramakrishna Math, No year of publication), p. ix.

[7] T.S. Narayana Aier, *The Age of Śaṅkara*, p. 33.

[8] Swami Tapasyananda in the "Introduction" to Madhva-Vidyaranya, *Śaṅkara-Dig-Vijaya,* p. xxiii.

and virtuous but short-lived one. He chose the latter.[9] This is how the life of Śaṅkara[10] had started. He was considered as no ordinary human being but the incarnation of Śiva – Lord Śiva comes with human flesh.

In his fifth year *Upanayana* ceremony was done for Śaṅkara and as early as at the age of eight he had finished his Vedic learning and return home from the house of his guru. His father was not fortunate enough to see his son's extraordinary skill and knowledge and his subsequent fame as he died when Śaṅkara was only three years old. Śaṅkara became a *Sannyāsin* after a reluctant mother who dares not lose his only son to asceticism was persuaded. Traditions of various sources were anonymous that he became the disciple of sage Govinda who was the disciple of the great Gaudapada, the founder of Vedānta philosophy. After several years of training under his guru, Śaṅkara departed from him for Varanasi (Benares) which was the center of religious learning and propagation during that time and stayed there for several years, gathering disciples and devoting to writing commentaries. Madhava maintains that it was his guru Govinda who sent him to Varanasi to proclaim the message of advaita, in spite of his desire to be with him and serve him throughout his life.[11] Tradition maintains that at Varanasi Śaṅkara was received a commission to proclaim the unity of reality to the whole country from Lord Śiva himself who appeared before him in disguise as a *Chandala* (out-caste).[12] He faithfully followed his Master's wish in bringing the gospel of unity of reality to the four corners of the country till his death at the early age of 32 or 38 according to some authorities.[13]

---

[9] T.M.P. Mahadevan, *Śaṅkarācharya*, (New Delhi: National Book Trust, India, 1968), pp. 4-5.

[10] His father gave him the name Śankara which means the bestower (*kara)* of happiness (*sam*), Cf. Madhva-Vidyaranya, *Śaṅkara-Dig-Vijaya: The Traditional Life of Sri Śaṅkarācharya*, p. 17.

[11] *Ibid.*, p. 56.

[12] *Ibid.*, p. 59.

[13] C.N. Krishnaswami Aiyer, "Life and Time of Śankara", in *Three Great Acharyas: Śaṅkara, Ramanuja, Madhwa*, p. 58.

1.3. His Works

Just like his life, there is confusion and contention concerning the works of Śaṅkara. There is huge literature piling up that bears the name of Śaṅkara. According to De Smet, who can be considered as one of the specialists in Śaṅkara's study, the list of the writings which bears the name of Śaṅkara comprises of 433 titles. Modern scholarship rejects most of these as spurious and recognises the following as the genuine Śaṅkara's works:[14]

(a) The commentary (*bhāṣya*) on nine Upaniṣads[15] – such as *Bṛhadāranyaka, Chāndogya, Aitareya, Taittīriya, Īśa, Kena, Kaṭha, Praśna and Muṇdaka*

(b) The commentary on *Bhagavad Gītā*

(c) The Commentary on *Brahma Sūtra* or *Vedānta Sūtra*

(d) A non-commentarial treatise – the *Upadeśa-Sāhasrī.*

2. The Main Teachings of Śankara

Śaṅkara's teachings presented by the Indologists and Indian scholars in a number of books are misleading as they misrepresented Śaṅkara's original teachings. Some of the most common misinterpretations of Śaṅkara's Advaita Vedānta includes – Brahman alone is real, the world is false, or the world is *māyā*, the illusory manifestation of Brahman, human soul is identical with Brahman, some of the Upaniṣadic statement like – *sarvam khalvidam Brahma* (verily this whole world is Brahman), *Aham Brahmāsmi* (I am Brahman) should be understood literally, Brahman is *nirguṇa* which means Brahman is impersonal so no proper personal relationship is possible with Brahman.[16] Another prominent mis-interpretation is that for Śaṅkara there is only one

---

[14] R. De Smet, "Śaṅkara's Non-dualism (Advaita-Vāda)", p. 82.

[15] Many scholars and even contemporary researcher put the total of Śaṅkara's commentary on Upaniṣad to ten. Cf. Roger Marcaurelle, *Freedom through Inner Renunciation: Śaṅkara's Philosophy in a New Light*, (Delhi: Sri Satguru Publications, 2002), p. 12.

[16] Cf. R. De Smet, "Śaṅkara's Non-dualism (Advaita-Vāda)", pp. 81-82.

genuine path for Self-realization, that is, *Jñāna* (knowledge) and that *Karma* (work) has no ontological value for humans' liberation.

Over against such misinterpretations, we make attempt here to present in brief the main theological teachings of Śaṅkara.

2.1. Brahman

According to Śaṅkara, Brahman is the non-dual *(A-dvaita)* absolute, who alone is Being (*sat*) in the supreme sense of the term (*paramārthatah*). He[17] cannot be expressed by the primary meaning (*mukhyārtha*) of words but only indicated (*lakṣita*) by the secondary meaning (*lakṣyārtha*) of terms.[18] For Śaṅkara the Upaniṣadic explanation of Brahman as *neti neti* designates that the Brahman unaffected by its *upādhis* (limiting adjuncts or extrinsic denominator) is beyond the grasp of speech and mind, "When, however, we wish to describe Its true nature, free from all differences due to limiting adjuncts, then it is an utter impossibility. Then there is only one way left, viz., to describe It as 'Not this, not this,' by eliminating all possible specifications of It that one may know of" (*Bṛ.U.B.* 2.3.6).[19]

However, indescribable He might be, Śaṅkara uses a number of adjectives to indicate Brahman, such as: Brahman is eternal, pure, intelligent, free by nature, all-knowing, all-powerful, unchangeably permanent, devoid of all modifications (*vikriyā*), partless (*niravayavam*), birthless (*ajaḥ*), undecaying (*ajaraḥ*), fearless (*abhayaḥ*), etc.[20]

---

[17] In this book, mostly masculine 'He' is used as personal pronounce for Brahman for convenience sake even though we acknowledge that Brahman is beyond sex as to be put as 'He'.

[18] K.P. Aleaz, *The Relevance of Relation in Śaṅkara's Advaita Vedānta*, (Delhi: Kant Publications, 1996), p. 27.

[19] Śaṅkara, *Bṛihadāraṇyaka Upaniṣad Bhāṣya*, translated by Swami Mahavananda; (Mayavati: Advaita Aśhrama, 1950), p. 344.

[20] Cf. K.P. Aleaz, *The Relevance of Relation in Śaṅkara's Advaita Vedānta*, pp. 37-38.

Śankara explains Brahman in relation to His creations as follows –

> Therefore, the unconditioned Self, being beyond speech and mind, undifferentiated and one is designated as "Not this not this"; when it has the limiting adjuncts of the body and organs which are characterized by ignorance, desire and work, it is called the transmigrating individual self; when the Self has the limiting adjuncts of the power of eternal and unlimited knowledge, it is called Internal Ruler and *Īsvara*. The same Self as by nature transcendent, absolute and pure, is called the Immutable and Supreme Self. Similarly, having the limiting adjuncts of the bodies and organs, the Undifferentiated, the gods, the species, the individual, men, animals, spirits, etc., the Self assumes those particular names and forms (*Bṛ.U.B.* 3.8.12).[21]

2.2. Human Being

According to Śaṅkara human being is nothing but Brahman with the *upādhis* (limiting adjuncts or extrinsic denominator) (*Bṛ.U.B.* 3.8.12),[22] or in other words the Self (*Ātman*) presiding over the cage of body and senses and associated with the fruit of action is called individual soul (*jīva*) (B.S.B 2.3.16).[23] So, it is cleared that though *jīva* is the prototype of Brahman, it is not identical with Brahman. A person is a *jīvātman* plus inner senses, outer senses and body conjoined. It is a reflection (*ābhāsa*) of the Supreme Ātman in the mirror-like ego-sense. As Brahman is real human being is also real, but its reality is derived from Brahman. Human being is not an illusion but an ontologically relative and dependent contingent entity. In other words, for Śaṅkara, human being is an

---

[21] Śaṅkara, *Bṛihadāraṇyaka Upaniṣad Bhāṣya*, pp. 528-529.

[22] *Ibid.,* p. 528.

[23] Śaṅkara, *Brahma Sūtra Bhāṣya*, translated by Swami Gambhirananda, (Calcutta: Advaita Aśhrama, 1993), p. 472.

integrated contingent being totally dependent on the Absolute, the Brahman.[24]

2.3. Creation

Śaṅkara says that Brahman created the entire universe in due order but without the help of any substance other than Himself. So, the whole universe is Brahman alone and is real but its reality is derived reality, derived from Brahman. The world originates, lives and is absorbed in Brahman. At all these three point of time, the world remains in Brahman. In other words, the entire universe is the *upādhis* of Brahman, the effect (*kārya*) and name and form (*nāma rūpa*) of Brahman.[25] As Brahman is real, His name and form which are His limited adjuncts should also be real. K.P. Aleaz notes, "Left to themselves, they are unreal. Our ignorance lies in identifying the extrinsic denominators as real in themselves."[26]

2.4. Māyā

One of the important themes of Śaṅkara's theology/philosophy which is widely misunderstood is his concept of *māyā* where many interpretations label that the world is *māyā*, the illusory manifestation of Brahman. But according to Śaṅkara, *māyā* "is the power of the Supreme Lord (*parameśvaryah śakteh*) ... which creates the whole universe (*samastajagadvidhāyinyā*)."[27] For Śaṅkara *māyā* does not mean total 'illusion' that makes the material world looks real, he calls the universe as the product of *māyā* only when it is misapprehended by the ignorant as independently real apart from Brahman.

2.5. Bondage and Liberation

The goal of Śaṅkara's theology/philosophy is the liberation of the bonded soul in order to regain its original purity. Śaṅkara himself

---

[24] K.P. Aleaz, *The Relevance of Relation in Śaṅkara's Advaita Vedānta*, pp. 27-28.

[25] *Ibid.*, p. 28.

[26] *Ibid.*, p. 50.

[27] *Ibid.*, p. 63.

attests thus, "There is no other attainment higher than that of the Self. For that is the purpose for which the teachings of the Vedas, the Śmṛitis and the actions (described in the work-portion of the Vedas) are there" (U.S.17.4).[28] Śaṅkara goes along with the general conception of transmigration of soul from one body to another – i.e. jīva transmigrates into another body at death. This is the result of the past accumulated actions, so the condition of the new body would also be determined by the past life. Śaṅkara is very specific that when the Self passes form one body to another there is no change in the Self (B.G.B. 2:13).[29] For Liberation to happen Śaṅkara suggests four things as a pre-requisites – (a) to get the help of a competent guru, (b) to learn and study Vedānta, (c) to be able to control senses (d) to be able to discriminate between what is real and what is unreal (B.G.B. 18.50).[30] For the realization of Brahman Śaṅkara prescribes *Karma yoga* and *Jñāna Yoga*; this is the thesis of this research which will be elaborated more in the following chapters.

3. Concluding Remarks

A brief survey on the life and teaching of Śaṅkara shows the helplessness of scholars and experts on Śaṅkara's life and philosophy in locating the truth about his life; the more we read the different accounts, the more confused we are. Few facts acceptable to most scholars concerning his life are so few that they are hardly enough to reconstruct meaningfully the life of Śaṅkara. The *Śankara-Vijayas* which are our only source for reconstructing Śaṅkara's life are also highly fanciful and whimsical that it is rather difficult to differentiate the truth from the legend. The same thing is felt when it comes to locating the authentic writings of Śaṅkara. Today's scholarship opines that Śaṅkara made commentaries on nine or ten principal *Upaniṣad*, *Brahma Sūtras* and *Bhagavad*

---

[28] Śaṅkara, *Upadeśa Sāhasrī*, translated by Swami Jagadananda, (Madras: Sri Ramakrishna Math, 1989), p. 192.

[29] Śaṅkarāchārya, *Bhagavad Gītā Bhāṣya*, translated by A. Mahadeva Shastri, (Mysore: Government Oriental Library, 1901), p. 25.

[30] *Ibid.*, p. 442.

Gītā. He also wrote a non-commentarial philosophical/theological treatise - *Upadeśa Sāhasrī*.

Śaṅkara stands for absolute oneness of reality, that Brahman alone is real. The world including human being is the name and form (*nāma-rūpa*), the limiting adjunct (*upādhi*) of Brahman. In that sense it is real, however, the reality of the world or human being is not independent reality, but derived reality, derived from Brahman. The world with all its diversity is real with Brahman, unreal without Brahman. The basic human problem consists in the identification of the soul with the material world due to ignorance. As ignorance is the primary cause, the removal is prescribed as knowledge. However, Śaṅkara does not negate the importance of Works (religious activities) but give more or less equal status with Knowledge as we shall see in the following chapters.

Chapter 2

Śankara's Theological Method

That Śaṅkara has been mis-read and mis-interpreted by many people, including those of his later followers, is a fact that is held by most of the contemporary scholars on Śaṅkara's Advaita Vedānta. There are various reasons as to why such misunderstandings and misinterpretations happened. *Firstly*, as pointed out earlier, Śaṅkara has been interpreted from various works ascribed to him which are not the genuine works of Śaṅkara; *secondly*, most of his works are commentarial treatise and lack systematic presentation; *thirdly*, he uses Sāṁkhya language of speculation without creating new terms to explain his position but it seems to be inadequate;[1] *lastly*, he follows a particular type of hermeneutical principle and many interpreters of Śaṅkara seem to have failed in recognizing it. Thus, a proper understanding of his method is a must for a correct understanding of his theology/philosophy.

---

[1] R. De Smet, "Śaṅkara's Non-dualism (Advaita-Vāda)", in *Religious Hinduism*, edited by R. De Smet and J. Neuner, Fourth Revised Edition, (Mumbai: St. Pauls, 1997), p. 81.

1. Śaṅkara – A *Śrutivādin*

There is hardly any room for misgiving that Śaṅkara is through and through a *Śrutivādin* – one who solely rely on the scripture for his philosophical or theological writings. This is self-evident when we read his voluminous commentaries. He has complete faith in the authority and infallibility of *Śruti*. He asserts time and again that his teaching is beyond the grasp of reason as it is entirely based on the testimony of the *Śruti*, the revealed scripture. He interprets scripture by scripture; verses of scripture are explained by using another verses.[2] As he depends on scripture rather than reason, Śaṅkara is more a theologian than a philosopher, his approach is theological rather than philosophical.

2. Sources of Valid Knowledge (*pramāṇas*)

Śaṅkara accepts six *pramāṇas* (sources of valid knowledge) such as Perception (*pratsyakṣa*), inference (*anumāna*), comparision (*upamāna*), verbal testimony, that is, scripture (*śabda*), presumption (*arthāpatti*) and negation (*abhāva*).[3] However, scripture (*śabda*) is always supreme. He does not accept the authority of all the scriptures, for him *Śruti* (Vedas) is the only valid scripture and the most reliable *pramāṇa*.

3. Śaṅkara's Hermeneutical Predisposition

Śaṅkara's writings can be divided into two catagories – *textual* and *para-textual*. 'Textual' is his direct commentary on the scriptural texts, it is all that depends directly on the texts he commended upon. 'Para-textual' is those of his personal predispositions, his opinions and principles which are at work while he comments a text but are not directly coming from the text itself. It is the manifestations of his mental clarity, his vast knowledge and intellectual genius

---

[2] K.P. Aleaz, *The Relevance of Relation in Śaṅkara's Advaita Vedānta*, (Delhi: Kant Publications, 1996), p. 25.

[3] Karl H. Potter, "Introduction to the Philosophy of Advaita Vedanta", in *Encyclopedia of Indian Philosophies: Advaita Vedānta up to Śaṁkara and His Pupils*, edited by Karl H. Potter, (Delhi: Motilal Banarsidass, 1981), p. 97.

coupled with his monastic experience.[4] It is considered that in the whole of his writings, it is the 'para-textual' that plays a pivotal role in determining Śaṅkara's theological position.

An ardent student of Śaṅkara's theology will be marvelled at his knowledge of the overall philosophical and religious thoughts that developed up to his time and that were prevalent during his time. His principle is clear as he puts it in his *Brahma Sūtra* Commentary - "the teaching of others, if not inconsistent with our own, becomes an accompaniment of our own thinking" (BSB 2.4.12). He studies other doctrines/philosophies with a discerning mind, takes what he feels is right, rejects and refutes what is wrong. Śaṅkara never rejects other doctrines unless and untill he studied them methodically to give a befitting refute and at the same time never misses to absorb the 'excellent' as he says in his commentary to Kaṭha Upaniṣad 2:2 – "The wise man sifts the excellent from the merely pleasant, going mentally all around these two objects, examining them closely, weighing their respective importance or futility, and having distinguished them he chooses the excellent alone on the account of its superiority". It was his practice that whenever he is going to refute any school of thought, be it Mīmāmsā, Jaina, etc., he would present the stand taken by that particular school in details, weighing their strengths and weaknesses and then only give his refutation.

For Śaṅkara, human beings are born with ignorance (*avidyā*) that makes them superimpose the nature of the Absolute upon the relative and *vice versa,* like taking a rope for a snake. However, humans have desire and capability for knowledge of Brahman which is *the goal of human* (*puruṣārtha*). Knowledge according to Śaṅkara is of two types – *Jñāna*, simple knowledge which is imparted to the students by the guru, and *vijñāna* – interiorized knowledge or truly discerning knowledge – the intuitive experiential knowledge. We need to possess *vijñāna*, but it is not possible without prior ascertaining of truth or unless we have what we called simple knowledge obtained from the teaching of the

[4] R. De Smet, "Śaṅkara's Non-dualism (Advaita-Vāda)", p. 83.

guru lest we will interiorize the untruth. For Sankara, the primary aim of his commentary is to give this prior ascertaining of truth.[5]

4. Śaṅkara's Hermeneutical Principle

Śaṅkara employs a particular type of hermeneutical principle, that is, the theory of implication (*lakṣaṇā*) or analogical function of words beyond their express meaning. It is his conviction that Brahman is beyond the expressive ability of human language, words and sentences. In other words Brahman cannot be expressed with words but can only be implied, our explanations whatever elaborate they might be, do not really express Brahman, but they just indicate or implied (*lakṣ-*) Brahman. "It is because it (Brahman) transcends the expressive power of all terms."[6] So, Śaṅkara uses the words of ordinary language according to some definite meaning of which he is perfectly aware. He means their express meaning (*mukhyārtha*) when the things he speaks of belong to the phenomenal realm (*vyavahāra*), but means their implied meaning (*lakṣyārtha*) when he talks about things of transcendental realm (*paramārtha*).[7] For example, the express meaning of the words such as *ātman* (self), *sat* (being/truth), etc., cannot be applied to the Absolute Brahman but their implied meaning has value to indicate Brahman. The express meaning of these words mean worldly beings, but these words in their secondary meaning – their implied meaning, no longer mean worldly beings. In other words, Brahman cannot be expressed by the primary meaning of the words but only indicate (*lakṣita*) by the secondary meaning. When Śaṅkara speaks from the Supreme standpoint his language is always of the latter kind.[8] Understanding the theory of implication (*lakṣaṇā*) as Śaṅkara applied it in his writings is a key to correctly interpret him. Most of the misinterpretations of Śaṅkara happened presumably due to the failure of recognising his usage of the *lakṣaṇā* principle.

---

[5] *Ibid.*, p. 84.

[6] *Ibid.*, p. 86.

[7] K.P. Aleaz, *The Relevance of Relation in Śaṅkara's Advaita Vedānta*, p. 26.

[8] *Ibid.*, pp. 26-27.

5. The Place of Śaṅkara in the Overall Methodological Issues in the Study of Religion

Śaṅkara, like all the Indian thinkers, does not care to distinguish philosophy from religion for the simple fact that these two are integrally related as he understood. In his philosophical discussion both reason and scripture play an important role. However, we may say that Śaṅkara falls into the category of Philosophical approach to the study of religion. But, it should be noted that he does not go along with the Western understanding of philosophy of religion where it is understood as a branch of philosophy. In his approach to religion or the doctrine of Self-Realization, Śaṅkara does not differentiate religion from philosophy, rather he integrated these two. His philosophy is theological and his theology is philosophical.

Another important feature of Śaṅkara's approach is the practical motif present in it. His philosophy does not end with theory or intellectual exercise, but rather the aim and goal of it is the upliftment of the ignorant souls to the level of liberation. For the ignorant to climb the ladder of spirituality so as to attain purity of mind, Śaṅkara endorses various types of rites and rituals. Once the mind is pure, man/woman is able to tread the path of knowledge which yields finally liberation. After liberation, he still prescribes the continuance of works for the benefit of the world. So, through and through, Śaṅkara philosophical approach is praxis oriented, aiming at practical benefits for the seekers. In other words, Śaṅkara's Advaita Vedānta is a philosophy of life and existence.

Śaṅkara's metaphysic primarily concerns the unity of human being with the Ultimate Reality; his epistemology includes both reason oriented *pramāṇas* such as perception, inference, comparison, presumption and negation as well as faith-oriented *pramāṇas* - *Sābda*, the verbal testimony. This is indicative of the integral relationship of between philosophy and religion in Śaṅkara's approach to the study of religion. The third division of his philosophy or theology, that is, Ethics concerns how human should live his/her life in accordance with the standard set by God;

it is the practical side of his philosophy/theology. So, Saṅkara's philosophy, like other Indian philosophies "is an applied religious discipline and not merely theoretical or contemplative one because it aims at concrete tangible result."[9]

Śaṅkara's emphasis on the integral relationship between philosophy and religion in the study of religion is reflected in his approach to salvation as well. He sees the importance of *Karma* (religious activities) and the indispensability of *Jñāna* (knowledge) for Self-realization. In his approach to salvation, he puts emphasis on the essential relationship between *Karma* and *Jñāna* as we shall see in the following discussion. This is a clear indication that Śaṅkara follows what we understand as an Indian conception of 'philosophical approach' to the study of religion with its distinctive characters, distinct from the Western notion of philosophy of religion.

---

[9] K.P. Aleaz, *Dimensions of Indian Religion: Study, Experience and Interaction*, (Calcutta: Punthi Pustak, 1995), p. 26.

Chapter 3

Śaṅkara's Interaction with the Mīmāmsā

Śaṅkara's writing has two basic purposes – one is to establish the oneness of reality over against duality as projected in Sāṃkhya system, and secondly, it is to refute Mīmāmsā system which ascribes Vedic ritual as the way to liberation for the bonded soul. In fact Śankara's main opposition was Mīmāmsākas. This Chapter deals in brief Śaṅkara's interaction with Mīmāmsā School in connection with the role of work (*karma*) for Self-realization. This is important in our research when we are trying to find the place of *karma* in Śaṅkara's Advaita Vedanta.

1. The Place of Works (*Karma*) in Mīmāmsā School

The Pūrva Mīmāmsā School of Jaimini (or 'Mīmāmsā School' as popularly known) is based on the ritualistic side of the Vedas. It lays great importance to the *Brāhmaṇas* than to the *Mantras* which means that it looks upon Vedas as essentially a book of ritual.[1] There are two ways by which Mīmāmsā tries to help and support

[1] M. Hiriyanna, *Outlines of Indian Philosophy*, (Delhi: Motilal Banarsidass, 2000), p. 299.

ritualism – (a) to supply methodological tools for understanding, harmonizing and following the complicated Vedic rituals, (b) to foster a philosophical justification of the beliefs on which ritualism depends.[2] To support its emphasis on ritualism, Mīmāmsā School claims that Vedas are eternal and self-existing and are not the handiwork of human beings - implying the necessity of following what are there in them. For Mīmāmsākas, human responsibility is to do his/her duty that includes ritual performance. However, "ritual enjoined by the Vedas should be performed not with the hope of any reward but just because they are so enjoined", because only "the disinterested performance of the obligatory rites… gradually destroys the *karmas* and bring about liberation after death."[3] Obligatory rite is to be performed not because it will benefit the performers, but it is because we ought to perform it as it is the injunction of the Vedas.[4] The Mīmāmsā also admits that when any person performs any ritual, there arises in his/her soul potency (*apūrva*) which produces in future the fruit of action that he or she will enjoy.[5]

In his commentary of Brahma Sūtra, Śaṅkara presents the stand taken by the Mīmāmsā School on the validity and importance of rites before he gives a refutation. We shall reproduce here the Mīmāmsākas's argument in favour of works (rites) provided to us by Śaṅkara himself and then give his refutation.

The Mīmāmsā School does not ignore the necessity of knowledge, but maintains that knowledge is subservient to rites and is part of the rites. They argue the validity of rites by stating that it is the injunction of Upaniṣads. A variety of Upaniṣadic texts show that rites are important – "Janaka, emperor of Videha, performed a sacrifice in which gifts were freely distributed" (Bṛ.U. 3.1.1), "Sir, I am about to perform a sacrifice" (Ch.U. 5.11.5). "If liberation

---

[2] Satischandra Chaterjee and Dhirendramohan Datta, *An Introduction to Indian Philosophy*, (Calcutta: University of Calcutta, 2004, Eight Edition), p. 313.

[3] *Ibid.*, p. 44.

[4] *Ibid.*, p. 337.

[5] *Ibid.*, p. 45.

can be achieved through knowledge alone, why should they have undertaken (the householder's) duties involving strenuous effort, for proverbially it is known, 'Why should one go to a hill if one has honey at hand'."[6] In other place the Upaniṣad declares that "rite becomes more powerful that is done along with meditation, faith, and sacred knowledge" (Ch.U. 1.1.10). Therefore, knowledge is heard of as forming a part of some rites hence knowledge by itself cannot be the cause of liberation. Knowledge cannot be independent in the text, "It (i.e. the departing soul) is followed by knowledge, work, (and past experience) (Bṛ.U. 4.4.2.), so, knowledge and work are seen to act in association in producing the result."[7]

Mīmāmsā maintains that according to Upaniṣad one who is possessed of the knowledge of all the things revealed in the Vedas is qualified for undertaking rites for it is said, "One who comes back from his teacher's house after duly reading (i.e. reciting) the Vedas… and then enters the householder's life and continues the study of the Vedas in a holy place and performs other prescribed duties, attains the world of Brahman" (Ch.U. 8.9.1). From this also it follows that knowledge cannot produce its result independently. That which is known as the *Agnihotra* is a sacrifice that has to be followed till decrepitude and death, for one gets released from it either through decrepitude or death. It follows that knowledge is a subsidiary of rites.[8]

From this it is cleared that Mīmāmsā School stands for three things in connection with the relationship between work and knowledge –

- Knowledge is part of rites,
- Knowledge alone does not produce liberation,
- Knowledge is in fact subservient to rites.

---

[6] *B.S.B.* 3.4.3. in Śaṅkara, *Brahma Sūtra Bhāṣya* (*B.S.B*), translated by Swami Gambhirananda, (Calcutta: Advaita Ashrama, 1993), p. 761.

[7] *B.S.B.* 3.4.4. & 3.4.5 in *Ibid.*, pp. 761-762.

[8] *B.S.B.* 3.4.6 and 3.4.7. in *Ibid.*, pp. 762-763.

Śaṅkara gives an elaborate refutation to this stand of Mīmāmsā School as we shall present here below.

2. Śaṅkara's Refutation to Mīmāmsā School

2.1. Śaṅkara starts his argument by pointing out that the thing to realized is much greater than the embodied soul, which is free from the mundane attributes as agenship – the Supreme Self, so His knowledge cannot supply any impulsion for work, on the contrary it uproots all works, because it is stated in the aphorism, "Knowledge is independent of rites, since it uproots all worldly distinctions."[9] So, what the teacher Bādarāyaṇa had expressed in Brahma Sūtra 3.4.1, "Liberation results from this knowledge of the Self, because the Vedic texts declare so" remains as it is, and it cannot be shaken by the fallacious arguments that knowledge is subsidiary of rites.[10]

2.2. The Mīmāmsā School's emphasis on works sprung from its belief that individual self is real in itself because the transmigrating soul is indicated by terms like "lovable", etc. Śaṅkara on the other hand, argues that this text should not be understood as referring to the absolute difference between the individual self and Brahman, for it is said "That thou art" (Ch.U. 6.8.7), "There is no other witness but this", etc. In its real nature, the embodied soul is but God Himself, while its state of embodiedness is a creation of limiting adjuncts.[11]

2.3. In reply to the stand taken by the Mīmāmsā School that for the enlightened humans it follows that knowledge is subservient to rites, Śaṅkara maintains, "Upaniṣadic mention of the conduct of enlightened men (*sic*) is equally in evidence to show that knowledge is not subservient to rites."[12] He quotes verses like, "The Kāvaṣeya seers who has known this very entity says, 'Why need we study, why need we perform sacrifices… the enlightened of yore ceased

[9] *B.S.B.* 3.4.8. in *Ibid.*, pp.763-764.

[10] *Ibid.*, p. 764.

[11] *Ibid.*

[12] *Ibid.*, p. 765.

to perform the *Agnihotra* sacrifice" (Kau. 2.5); "Knowing this very Self the Brāhmaṇas renounce the desires for sons, for wealth, and for worlds, and lead a mendicant life" (Bṛ.U. 3.4.1); "'This much indeed is immortality, my dear', saying this Yājñavalkya embraced a mendicant's life" (Bṛ.U. 4.5.15).[13] However, it is to be remembered that Śaṅkara never negates the importance of works even for the enlightened ones, on the contrary he suggests that the enlightened one may continue performing his/her usual acts for setting an example to others.[14]

2.4. In connection with the Upaniṣadic text that states: "That rites become more powerful that is done along with meditation, faith and secret knowledge" (Ch.U. 1.1.10) which the Mīmāmsākas take it as indicating the superiority of rite over knowledge, Śankara replies – this does not refer to all kinds of knowledge, it being confined to the relevant meditation that forms the topic. The topic under discussion there is the meditation on Udgītha as contained in, "One shall meditate on the letter *Om* as Udgītha" (Ch.U. 1.1.1).

2.5. Śaṅkara drives home his concluding part of the refutation by stating that knowledge is not inferior to rites, on contrary knowledge is by itself sufficient for liberation and in fact, is the only mean for attaining Brahman. But, rite (work) also has its own value – these two means: Knowledge and Work are but meant for two distinct people, the different stages of life. He says, "A division is to be noted here to the effect that knowledge follows one, and work another" (*B.S.B.* 3.4.11). Whereas knowledge applied mainly to the mendicants, works applied to the householders. But, he firmly believes that works (rites) do not produce the necessary result of liberation by *itself* whereas knowledge does; works leads to knowledge which finally leads to liberation. So, in a way rites are for the glorification of knowledge (*B.S.B.* 3.4.14). Works (rites)

---

[13] *B.S.B.* 3.4.9, in *Ibid.*

[14] Cf. B.G.B. 3.20 in Śaṅkarāchārya, *Bhagavad Gītā Bhāṣya*, translated by A. Mahadeva Shastri, (Mysore: Government Oriental Library, 1901), p. 93.

are useful for liberation in an indirect manner whereas knowledge has a direct result of producing the realization of Brahman.

Thus, knowledge cannot be a subsidiary of rites (*B.S.B.* 3.4.15). According to scriptures, knowledge destroys the whole world of manifestations which are the creation of ignorance as it is stated, "But when to the knower of Brahman everything has become the Self, then what should one smell and trough what", and so on (Bṛ.U. 2.4.14). So, this also follows that knowledge is independent of rites (*B.S.B.* 3.4.16). According to Śaṅkara as knowledge belongs to the monks (the final stage of *Aśrama Dharma*), knowledge cannot become subsidiary to rites since in that order rites are absent as the monks are not required to perform Vedic rites like *Agnihotra*, etc. Monasticism is not only meant for the last stage of life, but for all stages of life according to the individual commitment (cf. Ch.U. 2.23.1; Ch.U. 5.10.1; Mu.U. 1.2.11; Bṛ. 4.4.22; Jābāla 4), for this reason also knowledge is independent of rites (*B.S.B.* 3.4.17).

2.6. Finally, Śaṅkara comes to the concluding section of his refutation by stating the value and necessity of religious activities like rites, etc., thereby highlighting the integral relationship between *Karma* (work) and *Jñāna* (knowledge) for self-realization. He says, "Knowledge needs the help of all the duties of the various stages of life, and it is not a fact that there is absolutely no dependence on them" but "once knowledge has emerged, it does not depend on any other factor for producing its (own) result (viz. liberation); but it does depend on others for its own emergence."[15] He continues,

> On the strength of the Upaniṣadic texts prescribing sacrifice etc. Thus there occurs the text, "The Brāhmaṇas seek to know it through the study of Vedas, sacrifices, charity, austerity consisting in a dispassionate perception of sense object" (Bṛ. 4.4.22), which shows the helpfulness of sacrifices, etc., to the attainment of knowledge. Moreover, it is understood from their

[15] *B.S.B.* 3.4.26 in *Ibid.*, p. 781.

> association with "seeking to know" (Bṛ. 4.4.22), that they act as a means for the emergence of knowledge... the duties of the different stages of life are helpful to the acquisition of knowledge. *Smṛti* texts also support this, for instance, "The duties result in scorching away sins; the supreme goal being knowledge, when sins are scorched by duties, knowledge begins to emerge", and so on.[16]

The integral relationship between *jñāna yoga* and *karma yoga* is further explicated by Śaṅkara in the following lines –

> And in the Gītā and other *Smṛti* it has been stated elaborately that sacrifices, etc., when performed without any motive for fruits, become the means for the attainment of knowledge by an aspirant who desire liberation. Hence sacrifices, etc., and self control, etc., which are the duties of the respective stages of life, are all but means for the emergence of knowledge. And yet among these, such means as self-control, etc., which are connected with knowledge by the clause, "He who knows it as such" (Bṛ. 4.4.23), are proximate to knowledge, while the other means, viz., sacrifices, etc., are external (i.e. remote), they being connected with the seeking to know (Bṛ. 4.4.22). This is how these are to be distinguished.[17]

3. Concluding Remarks

Śaṅkara's refutation to the Mīmāmsā School concerning the role of rites consists of him stating the position of Mīmāmsā first and reacting to its teachings by using the various verses of the scripture. The main position of Mīmāmsā School is that rites are superior to knowledge which is but a part of rites and that knowledge alone does not produce the needed result, i.e., liberation and is subservient to rites. Śaṅkara gives elaborate reply to this and

[16] *B.S.B.* 3.4.26 in *Ibid.*, p. 783.

[17] *B.S.B.* 3.4.27 in *Ibid.*, p. 785.

maintains that knowledge is independent of rites and produces the needed result of liberation all by itself once it is emerged. It is neither part of the rites nor inferior to rites but is the only mean for attaining Brahman which is beyond the grasp of visible external human religious practices like rites, etc. He makes a distinction between works and knowledge by stating that they are meant for two separate classes of people; work is assigned mainly to the householders whereas knowledge is for the mendicants.

However, Śaṅkara does not neglect to relate these two – work and knowledge but maintains that knowledge, though it needs no help when it is emerged, alone could not lead people to liberating stage without the help of work. The importance and necessity of rites, therefore, is to elevate the seekers to a stage where they could be fit for knowledge to attain Brahman. Work has no direct excess to liberation and knowledge, though has direct access to liberation, needs the help of work for its emergence. Thus, according to Śaṅkara, *Jñāna Yoga* and *Karma Yoga* have integral relationship for the realization of Brahman. This point will be further explicated in the following chapters.

Chapter 4

Śaṅkara's Interpretation of the *Karma Yoga* of the Bhagavad Gītā

The previous Chapter partially deals with Śaṅkara's understanding of *Karma Yoga* which he presented by way of refuting Mīmāmsā's emphasis on rites in his commentary on *Brahma Sūtras*. This Chapter will throw more lights on this issue. Here, our discussion will be based on Śankara's *Bhagavad Gītā Bhāṣya*[1] from which we try to have a fuller picture of what has been discussed so far concerning the place of Works (Rites, etc.) in Śaṅkara's Advaita Vedānta. First sections deals with his endorsement of the twofold Vedic *dharma* – the religion of works and the religion of knowledge, second section talks about the validity of *Karma Yoga* and in the third section we discuss the place he assigns to *Karma Yoga* for Self-realization.

[1] In this paper we use Śaṅkarāchārya, *Bhagavad Gītā Bhāṣya*, translated by A. Mahadeva Shastri, (Mysore: Government Oriental Library, 1901) as our source.

1. The Two-Fold Vedic *Dharma*

Śaṅkara declares right from the beginning of his Bhagavad Gītā *Bhāṣya* that he admits the twofold Vedic Religion – *Pravṛitti Dharma* (the religion of works) and *Nivṛitti Dharma* (the religion of renunciation) and says, "It was the twofold Vedic Religion of Works and Renunciation that maintains order in the universe."[2] According to Śaṅkara, this twofold religion was taught by the Supreme Lord to Arjuna, who was deeply plunged in the ocean of grief and dilution, evidently thinking that the Religion would widely spread when accepted and practised by men and women of high character. Eventually, the Gītā *Sāstra* expounds this twofold religion with the aim of achieving the Supreme Bliss for the seekers.[3]

Śaṅkara maintains that both of these two means lead to the Supreme Bliss. He says that the religion (*dharma*) which consists in a steady devotion to the knowledge of the Self, preceded by the renunciation of all works leads to the Supreme Bliss. The religion of works which leads the devotees to the religion of the Devas, when practiced in a spirit of complete devotion to the Lord without expecting the results, it conduces to the purity of mind (*sattva-suddhi*). The man/woman whose mind is pure is competent to tread the path of knowledge, and to him/her comes knowledge. Thus, the Religion of Works forms also a means to the Supreme Bliss.[4] Śaṅkara consistently maintains throughout his works that Religion of Works (rites) and Religion of Renunciation (knowledge) have their place in the overall religious practices of the people.

These two means (or two types of religions) are for two different types of people. He says, "The Lord has made a distinction between *Jñana-niṣṭhā* and *Karma-niṣṭhā*, between the devotion of knowledge and the devotion of works as based respectively upon two distinct standpoints: *Sāṇkhya* Standpoint (*Sāṇkhya-buddhi*)

[2] *Ibid.*, p. 2.

[3] *Ibid.*, pp. 4, 6.

[4] *Ibid.*, pp. 5-6.

and Yoga Standpoint (*Yoga-buddhi*). The real nature of the Self is called *Sānkhya*, the intellectual conviction of the truth produced by a study that the Self is no doer, no birth, etc., forms the *Sāṇkhya* standpoint; whereas *Yoga* consists in the performance of works as a means to *mokṣa*, requiring a knowledge of virtue and sin, and presupposing that the Self is distinct from the body and is the doer and the enjoyer. Such a conviction forms the *Yoga* standpoint.[5] Śaṅkara states in his introduction to the second chapter of the Gītā thus:

> Accordingly two distinct standpoints are referred to by the Lord in 2:39. Of these, He will assign to the Sāṇkhyas the *Jñāna-yoga* or devotion to knowledge, based upon the Sāṇkhya standpoint; and so also He will assign to the *Yogins* the path of *Karma Yoga*, or devotion to works based upon the Yoga standpoint (3:3). Thus with reference to the Sāṇkhya and the Yoga standpoints two distinct paths have been shown by the Lord seeing the impossibility of *Jñāna* and *Karma* being conjoined in one and the same person simultaneously… Thus the Vedic rites are intended for him only who has desires and has no knowledge of the Self. The renunciation of these is enjoined on him who seeks only the region of the Self and is free from desire. This assigning of the two paths to two distinct classes of people would be unjustifiable if the Lord had intended a simultaneous conjunction of knowledge and Vedic rites.[6]

He says that this twofold religion or two means of salvation has been taught not only by the Lord but also by sage Vyāsa who said to his son, "Now there are two paths". For Vyāsa the part of works is first, and that renunciation comes next.[7]

---

[5] *Ibid.*, pp. 17-18.

[6] *Ibid.*, pp. 18-19.

[7] *Ibid.*, p. 38.

2. The Validity of Work for Self-realization in Saṅkara's Thought

A simple statement of Śaṅkara such as '*mokṣa* can be obtained by knowledge alone' misguided many scholars to think that for Śaṅkara Knowledge (*Jñāna Yoga*) is the *only way* for Self-realization. However, it is very clear that he believes that there *two ways* for salvation as he says in connection with whether these two ways should be conjoined or not: "If it had been meant that knowledge and action should be conjoined, then the means of salvation would be one only, and in that case, a groundless separation of knowledge from action would have been made by Arjuna declaring knowledge to be superior to action" (*B.G.B.* 3:1). It is also found in a number of places where he mentions that two ways are prescribed: "Twofold Vedic religion – religion of works and renunciation" (*B.G.B. Introduction*), "The Lord has made a distinction between *Jñāna-niṣṭhā* and *Karma-niṣṭhā* (*B.G.B.* 2:1-10); The Lord distinguishes between Yoga and Sāṇkhya (*B.G.B.* 2:39); "You are qualify for works alone not for the path of knowledge" (*B.G.B.* 2:47); "What was that twofold path of devotion? – One of them was *Jñāna-yoga*, the devotion of acknowledge...The other was *karma-yoga*, the devotion of action" (*B.G.B.* 3:3); "They (works and knowledge) produce but one harmonious result... Both lead to the same result, i.e., *mokṣa*" (*B.G.B.* 5:4), etc. So, there is no doubt that Śaṅkara believe in the validity of *Karma Yoga* as a mean for Self-realization.

So, Śaṅkara admits that performance of action eventually leads to *mokṣa*, he says, "Performing action, without attachment, for the sake of the *Iśvara*, man (*sic*) attains *mokṣa*, through attaining purity of mind (*sattva-suddhi*)" (*B.G.B.* 3:19). Works is not only important for the ignorant to attain perfection, but also indispensable for the one who had attained perfection to do for the benefit of the masses. "If though art ignorant, do thou perform action to purify the self. If thou art wise and knowest the truth, do thou perform action for the protection of masses. It was performed by the ancients such as Janaka in the olden time: it is not a recent instruction" (*B.G.B.* 4:15).

Thus, when Śaṅkara is studied comprehensively from his authentic works, without emphasizing one and neglecting the other, we grasp the beauty of his theology/philosophy - the comprehensive understanding of his prescribed methods for the liberation of human being. He maintains a balance, an equilibrium between the two paths/means which he says was taught by God Himself – the path of Knowledge and the path of Works. He did does not shy from saying, "Both lead to the same result, viz., *mokṣa*. Wherefore, there is no diversity in result" (*B.G.B.* 5:4).[8]

3. The Place Assigned for Works (*Karma Yoga*)

That Śaṅkara upholds in his Commentary to Bhagavad Gītā through and through that there are two means/paths for liberation – knowledge (*jñāna*) and work (*karma*) is established in the above discussion. Following this he says that these two paths should not be conjoined as they are different and distinct, conjunction is not possible,[9] and he even argues to the extent that if it is to be conjoined, these paths will be one, not two; the fact that they are made two negates the possibility of conjunction (*B.G.B.* 3:1). These two paths – *Jñāna Yoga* and *Karma Yoga* are for two distinct classes of aspirants. *Jñāna Yoga* is only for those who are wise and enlightened[10]; it is for the *Sānkhyas*, for those who possessed a clear knowledge of the Self and the not-Self, who renounced the world from *Brahmacharya*, who belonged to the highest class of *sannyāsins* known as the *Paramahansas*, whose thought ever dwelt on Brahman only (*B.G.B.* 3:3). It is evident that this path is not intended for a common people, but for *sannyāsins* only as Śaṅkara says, "It must also be true that the path of knowledge is intended from *Sannyāsins* only" (*B.G.B.* 3:3).[11] If it is so, does it mean that for Śaṅkara, householders or people in other stages of life (*Aṣramas*) have no hope for salvation unless and until they reach the stage of *sannyāsya* or complete renunciation? The

---

[8] *Ibid.*, p. 146.

[9] *Ibid.*, pp. 19, 72, 77-78, 80, 456-457.

[10] *Ibid.*, p. 38.

[11] *Ibid.*, p. 82.

answer is found when he said that Janaka and Asvapati who did not renounce their householder duties but "tried by action alone to attain *mokṣa*" were still considered as liberated[12]; that shows the possibility of salvation for the householder; or in other words, physical renunciation of all actions is not mandatory for attaining Brahman because, salvation is attainable by those who are actively doing their duties.

Śaṅkara's position is that these two means is for separate classes of people – *Jñāna yoga* is for the *sannyāsins* who renounced physically the world, and *Karma yoga* is for the rest of the stages, especially the householder, who while performing their holder duties tread the path of salvation via *Karma Yoga.*[13] He also says, "The *Karma-yoga*, devotion to action, is indeed meant for the ignorant only, not for the wise."[14] In that case, *Karma yoga* is also a valid path of salvation. However, Śaṅkara maintains that *Karma yoga,* i.e., Works (Vedic rites) *by itself* cannot lead people to a liberating stage. In other words, Work cannot lead directly to liberation but Works eventually leads to the discipline of knowledge which produces purity of mind that begets Self-knowledge which yields liberation. Here, Roger Marcaurelle is worth quoting:

> From Śaṅkara's perspective, even though the yoga of action cannot lead directly to liberation by reason of its basic involvement with the sense of doership, nevertheless, since it can be accompanied by the discipline of knowledge, together with the latter, it can produce the purity necessary for the mind to access, trough the scriptures, that experiential steadfastness in Self-knowledge (*jñānaniṣṭhā*), which alone is free from doership and yield liberation.[15]

---

[12] *Ibid.*, p. 92, cf. p. 22.

[13] *Ibid.*, pp. 85, 90.

[14] *Ibid.*, p. 85.

[15] Roger Marcaurelle, *Freedom through Inner Renunciation: Śaṅkara's Philosophy in a New Light*, (Delhi: Sri Satguru Publications, 2002), pp. 129-130.

So, according to Śaṅkara *Karma Yoga* in *itself* does not yield liberation directly, but if practiced without expecting the result (*niskāma karma*), it conduces purity of mind which in turn gives way for knowledge to spring resulting into liberation.

Works is not only a means of liberation, but also important even after attainment of liberation. The wise *kśatriyas* Janaka and Asvapati had been engaged in works and tried to reach *mokṣa* with action, i.e., without abandoning action with a view to set example to the world. These people perform actions not only for their salvation, but continue to do so for the welfare of the people (*B.G.B.* 3:20). So, if anyone thinks that he/she has achieved his/her ends and has realized the Self, "even he (*sic*) should work for the welfare of others, though for himself he (*sic*) may have nothing to do."[16] Śaṅkara's approval of works is vividly displayed here when he insists that works should be performed even after attaining *mokṣa*. "For me, or any other person who, knowing the Self, thus seeks the welfare of the world, there is nothing to do except it be with a view that welfare of the world at large… What then should he do? – Himself doing diligently and well the actions which the ignorant have to do, he should make them do these actions" (*B.G.B.* 3:25-26).

4. Concluding Remarks

Knowledge being assigned primary and most important place for Self-realization in Saṅkara's thought is beyond contestation, but Works is *not* un-important, let alone rejected for the attainment of Brahman. Moreover, Works is indispensable for the overwhelming majority of the seekers as they are not qualified to tread the path of knowledge for this path is assigned, in Śaṅkara's thought, to the *sannyāsin* alone.

As Śaṅkara identifies twofold Vedic religion – religion of Works and religion of Renunciation of Works (Knowledge) as authentic – the God-ordained *Dharma* for the people, the value and validity of *Karma-yoga* is self-revealed. These two means of salvation is distinct and cannot be conjoined as they are meant for

[16] *B.G.B.* 3:24 in *Ibid.*, p. 95.

two different classes of aspirants. However, Śaṅkara is firm in his stand that *Karma-yoga* (Vedic rites, etc.) alone could not itself lead the seeker-after-liberation to *mokṣa*, but *niskāma karma* (works without attachment or selfish motives) when constantly practiced will yield purity of mind (*sattva buddhi*). A person who is pure in mind is eligible to tread the path of knowledge and eventually he/she will be liberated. So, especially for the householder (*gṛhastha*), though knowledge is finally the thing that liberates, *Karma-yoga* is an indisputable path to follow for Self-realization, because the final stage in the journey for salvation is reached only when the preceding steps are trodden. Here comes the integral relationship between Works and Knowledge for Self-realization – even though they are distinct and should not be conjoined, these two paths helps each other, work together and are inseparably related for the liberation of human being. This will be further discussed in the next Chapter.

Chapter 5

Integral Relationship between *Karma* and *Jñāna* for Self-realization

Śaṅkara's recognition of the twofold *Vedic dharma* – religion of works and religion of knowledge has been established in the previous discussion, the validity of *Karma-yoga* as a means of salvation has also been ascertained, and the impossibility of conjoining these two paths as they are distinct parts meant for different group of seekers, is also well attested. The question now is whether these two are related or not, if so, to what extent they are related and this Chapter is trying to throw some lights on these issues.

1. *Jñāna-yoga* Superior to *Karma-yoga*

Even though Śaṅkara acknowledges two distinct means of salvation, he retains through and through that *Jñāna* is superior to *Karma* due to the fact that ultimately it is *Jñāna* that liberates and not *Karma*. This is because of the nature of liberation itself; since liberation is the same as Brahman, "It is not proper to talk of Brahman as though it formed a factor in some action" (*B.S.B.* 1.1.4), or "Liberation is the state of identity with Brahman and hence it is not to be achieved through purification" of body, mind or soul by means of works. So, "apart from knowledge alone, there cannot be the slightest touch of action here" (*B.S.B.* 1.1.4). Śaṅkara also writes: "The destruction (of ignorance) is possible by means of knowledge only, which is incompatible with ignorance."[1] In his commentary to Bhagavad Gītā, Śaṅkara also states, "Devotion to action is a mean to the end, not directly, but only leading to devotion to knowledge; whereas the latter, which is attained by means of devotion to action, leads to the goal directly, without extraneous help" (*B.G.B.* 3:3). In the other place he also says, "Pure Self-Knowledge alone is the means to the Highest Bliss... neither by works alone, nor by works and knowledge conjoined together is the Highest Bliss attained. Since, moreover, the Highest Bliss is not an effect to be accomplished by action, works cannot be the means to it."[2]

Therefore, Śaṅkara's stand is clear: *Jñāna-yoga* and 'not' *Karma-yoga* is ultimately the mean for Self-Realization. However, time and again, Śaṅkara also stated in his commentaries that two paths for salvation is guaranteed by the scriptures and that the Lord sets twofold Vedic religion – religion of works and religion of knowledge which are distinct from each other and meant for two different classes of aspirants. In the concluding portion of his Bhagavad Gītā Commentary, Śaṅkara makes a meaningful remark:

> It has been said "Knowing which one attains the Immortal" (13:12), and "Then knowing Me in truth, he forthwith enters into Me" (13:55): these and other passages teach that the Highest Bliss is attained by mere knowledge. Such passages again as "Thy concern

[1] U.S. 17:7 in Śaṅkarāchārya, *Upadeśa Sāhasrī*, translated by Swami Jagadananda, (Madras: Sri Ramakrishna Math, 1989), p. 193.

[2] Śaṅkarāchārya, *Bhagavad Gītā Bhāṣya*, translated by A. Mahadeva Shastri, (Mysore: Government Oriental Library, 1901), p. 455.

is with action alone" (2:47), and "Do thou also perform action" (4:15) teach that performance of works is quite obligatory.[3]

This follows that for Śaṅkara both knowledge and works are obligatory. The question now is - Is these two related? If so, in what way they are related?

2. The Relationship between *Jñāna* and *Karma*

Śaṅkara maintains that knowledge and works are two distinct paths and cannot be combined together in a person at the same time. Again, knowledge and works are for two different types of aspirants. It is the teaching of the Lord "that knowledge and action are intended for two distinct classes of men respectively on the ground that a simultaneous devotion – on the part of one man – to knowledge and action was impossible owing to their mutual opposition."[4] So, the path of knowledge is assigned to the wise such as *sannyāsins* whereas the path of *karma* is assigned to the ignorant persons. Prithipal notes, "It is true that the path of knowledge is prescribed for the *Sannyāsin* and that of action for the man still bound to discharge his social duties. But devotion to action is a means to an end."[5]

These two paths are designed in accordance with the phenomenal and absolute reality of the world and Brahman respectively. *Karma* is valid insofar as the phenomenal reality of this world is concerned whereas *Jñāna* is applicable to the absolute reality of Brahman. From the transcendental standpoint (*pāramārthika*) when we look at Brahman as the sole reality which is undifferentiated, immutable, etc., works (rites, etc.) has no actual significance because in Brahman there can be no activity. But from the perspective of phenomenal realm or common sense-viewpoint (*vyāvahārika*) when the world is considered as real because of

[3] *Ibid.*, pp. 454-455.

[4] *Ibid.*, p. 78.

[5] D. Prithipal, *Advaita Vedānta: Action and Contemplation*, (Varanasi: Bharatiya Vidya Prakasan, 1969), p. 55.

itself being in Brahman as Brahman is real, the worship of Īśvara with rites and rituals is considered to be significant, important and obligatory. Thus, states Śaṅkara, "Now, listen to the teaching concerning *Yoga* (path of works), which is the means of attaining wisdom concerning *Sāṇkhya* (path of knowledge): this *yoga*, which constitutes the worship of Īśvara, consists in practicing *Samādhi* or in performing works without attachment, after killing the pairs of opposites (such as heat and cold)" (*B.G.B.* 2:39).

Performance of rites is obligatory before the dawn of knowledge, and as long as humans are in the stage of ignorant. "A man who is qualifies for works it is necessary to perform works before he becomes fit for the path of knowledge" (*B.G.B.* 2:46). The positive aspect of Śaṅkara's teaching on *Karma-yoga* is that it purifies the mind so that it makes the devotees qualify to tread the path of *Jñāna-yoga*. K.N. Tiwari may be worth quoting, "Śaṅkara accepts the purificatory function of *karmas* without which the spiritual attainment is regarded as impossible. The Vedānta does not go further than that, but restricts the role of *karma* to the purificatory level."[6] In this sense, *Jñāna-yoga* and *Karma-yoga* work together for the liberation of human soul. Tiwari continues, "However paradoxical it may sound, yet it is eminently true that freedom from action is attained by the right performance of action (*B.G.B.* 3:3). Mere renunciation of action, i.e., simple and total inaction, is not in any way conducive to adherence to the path of knowledge."[7] In other words, renunciation of works is attained only when the devotee performs selfless and pure action. So, works and knowledge, though recognized as distinct means of salvation, is integrally related. Here, A.G. Krishna Warrier who had earned doctoral degree for his research on Saṅkara's concept of *Mukti* is worth quoting, he says, "Commenting on *Brahmasūtra* III.4.26 Śaṅkara discusses the important question of the relation between action and knowledge. Without performance of actions of

---

[6] Kapil N. Tiwari, *Dimensions of Renunciation in Advaita Vedānta*, (Delhi: Motilal Banarsidass, 1977), p. 85.

[7] *Ibid.*, p. 56.

four stations in life, the saving knowledge of identity cannot dawn at all; for thus alone the mind becomes fit for such knowledge."[8]

The birth of human is the consequence of the past *Karmas* which is due to *avidya* (ignorance) and therefore, any child being born is born with ignorance. So, according to Śaṅkara, every human being has to start his/her religious journey towards the end, i.e., liberation with rites and rituals (Works) as he/she is not fit for the higher path – path of Knowledge. But, works alone cannot liberate human, only in company with knowledge works has liberative capacity. When knowledge dawns in an individual, because of the purity of mind resulted from the works done without attachment, liberation is enhanced. Towards the end of his Commentary on Bhagavad Gītā, in a form of conclusion, Śaṅkara makes an important statement thus:

> Our theory moreover, does not drive us to the conclusion that the *sṛuti* teaching works proves useless; for by restraining the first natural activities one by one and thereby gradually inducing fresh and higher activities, it serves to create an aspiration to reach the Innermost Self. Though the means is *mithya* or illusory, still it is true, because the end is true … We may argue that the *sṛuti* treating of works is an authority in itself under other circumstances (i.e. before the attainment of Self-knowledge), just as *pratyakṣa* or sense-perception caused by attachment to the body is held to be authoritative prior to (the attainment of) Self-Knowledge.[9]

In support of the integral relationship between *Jñāna* and *Karma*, Śaṅkara makes a number of statements in his commentaries; few of them may be furthered here as follows: -

[8] A.G. Krishna Warrier, *The Concept of Mukti in Advaita Vedānta*, (Madras: University of Madras, 1981), p. 432.

[9] Śaṅkarāchārya, *Bhagavad Gītā Bhāṣya*, pp. 470-471.

"And in the Gītā and other *Smṛti* it has been stated elaborately that sacrifices, etc., when performed without any motive for fruits, become the means for the attainment of knowledge by an aspirant who desire liberation" (*B.S.B.* 3.4.27).

"Knowledge needs the help of all the duties of the various stages of life, and it is not a fact that there is absolutely no dependence on them" but "once knowledge has emerged, it does not depend on any other factor for producing its (own) result (viz. liberation); but it does depend on others for its own emergence" (*B.S.B.* 3.4.26).

"'On the strength of the Upaniṣadic texts prescribing sacrifice etc'. Thus there occurs the text, 'The Brāhmaṇas seek to know it through the study of Vedas, sacrifices, charity, austerity consisting in a dispassionate perception of sense object' (Bṛ.U. 4.4.22), which shows the helpfulness of sacrifices, etc., to the attainment of knowledge. Moreover, it is understood from their association with 'seeking to know' (Bṛ.U. 4.4.22), that they act as a means for the emergence of knowledge... the duties of the different stages of life are helpful to the acquisition of knowledge" (*B.S.B.* 3.4.26).

"Work helps from a distance (i.e. indirectly) in producing the result. As work leads gradually to knowledge, it is said by courtesy to lead to liberation itself. Accordingly, the statement that knowledge and work produce the same result refers to the work that had preceded knowledge" (*B.S.B.* 4.1.16).

"The obligatory rites like *Agnihotra,* etc., both as associated and unassociated with meditation, that were undertaken either in this life or the previous life before the dawn of knowledge, with a view to attaining liberation by one who hankers after it, become the destroyer as far as possible of the accumulated sins that stand in the way of the realization of Brahman. Thus indirectly they become the cause of realization of Brahman Itself, so that in collaboration with such proximate causes of enlightenment as hearing, reflection, faith, meditation, devotedness, etc., they come to have the same result as the knowledge of Brahman has" (*B.S.B.* 4.1.18).

"Devotion to action is a means to the end, nor directly, but only as leading to devotion to knowledge; whereas the latter, which is attained by means of devotion to action, leads to the goal directly, without extraneous help" (*B.G.B.* 3:3).

"Action... conduces to the destruction of sins committed in the past and cause purity of mind (*sattva, antaḥ-karaṇa*); and by thus purifying mind, they cause knowledge to spring up and lead to the path of devotion to knowledge... By abstaining from action man cannot attain to actionlessness (*niṣkarmya*), freedom from activity, i.e., devotion in the path of knowledge... From the statement that man wins not freedom from activity by abstaining from action, it is understood that by the opposite course, i.e., by performing action, man attains freedom from activity." So, performance of action is the means of attaining freedom from activity so also "devotion to action is the means of attaining devotion to knowledge". "In the *sṛuti*, for instance, *karma-yoga* is declared to be a means to *jñāna-yoga* in the following passage: "The Brahmaṇas seek to know this (the Self) by the study of the Vedas, by *yajña* or worship' (*Bṛ.U.* 4.4.22). In this passage, *karma-yoga* is pointed as a means of realizing the Self that is sought after" (*B.G.B.* 3:4).

> "The knowledge of the Absolute Reality arises when the mind is purified by *Karma Yoga*" (*B.G.B.* 2:51).

The above statement of Śaṅkara and many more may be cited in order to show the integral and inseparable relationship between *Karma-yoga* and *Jñāna-yoga* for Self-realization. Here, Subrahmanya Iyer is worth quoting when he says,

> The best interpretation of Śaṅkara's philosophy is that furnished by his own life which illustrates how action (*Karma*) and Thought (*Jñāna*) are "inseparable," and that *Jñāna* (thought, wisdom or philosophy) does not "in the least" imply inaction nor does "*mithyatwa*" (illusoriness) justify indifference to life, or callousness...he never sought any cave or temple or monastery for refuge or retirement or mystic realization, as so many *Yogis*, *Sadhus* and *Sannyāsis* do. He was 'ever' moving about the whole continent of India, 'organizing' and 'teaching,' with a view to helping all men to realise the underlying oneness or 'unity.'[10]

3. Concluding Remarks

By way of concluding our discussion on the integral relationship between *Karma-Yoga* and *Jñāna-Yoga* for Self-realization in Śaṅkara's thought, few emerging insights may be put forward here –

Firstly, there are two paths for human being to tread for attainment of the Self – the path of Works (*Karma-yoga*) and the path of knowledge (*Jñāna-yoga*). These are two distinct paths which are meant for two different classes of people and cannot be conjoined in one person at one time.

Secondly, the path of Works, which is operated in the phenomenal realm, consists in the worship of Īśvara with rites,

[10] V. Subrahmanya Iyer, "Śankara's Philosophy and Action" in *http://www.yabaluri.org/TRIVENI/CDWEB/ShankarasPhilosophyandAction1941.htm* (22.11.2011).

etc., and is meant for the ignorant before the dawn of knowledge. This path is valid because for the ignorant, who are not eligible to tread the path of knowledge, this is their *only* path that will lead them to purity of mind thereby making them eligible to tread the path of knowledge. The path of knowledge is for the wise, the *sannyāsins* and is the direct mean of liberation.

Thirdly, though these two paths are distinct, they are *not* unrelated. They need each other. *Karma* needs the accompany of *Jñāna* in order to reach the end – Self-realization, likewise *Jñāna* also needs *karma* for its own emergence, once knowledge has emerged, it does not depend on any other factor for producing its result, viz., liberation, but it does depend on others for its own emergence. It is clearly pointed out that action, not inaction, is solely responsible for the emergence of actionlessness, i.e., the path of Knowledge. In other words, Works (rites, etc.) helps the ignorant to climb the spiritual ladder towards perfection and finally produces purity of mind which is necessary for anyone to be able to tread the path of knowledge. This is so as to say that without Works, there can be no Knowledge, without actions salvation is unachievable as all are born ignorant and impure because birth itself is the product of *avidya* (ignorance).

Therefore, even though these two – *Works* and *Renunciation of Works* (knowledge) appear opposing one another, but in functional reality they are integrally related, complementing each other for the attainment of Brahman. It is not wise to try to deduce which one is more important let alone rejecting one in our emphasizing of the other as many scholars do. So, according to Śankara, these two – *works* and *knowledge* should be taken together as mutually collaborating for the production of the intended result, i.e., Self-realization.

Conclusion

This research has one basic intention, viz., to find out the integral relationship between *Karma Yoga* and *Jñāna Yoga* for Self-realization in Śaṅkara's Advaita Vedānta. Our approach is broadly scriptural or theological as we look mainly Śaṅkara's commentaries of scriptures like Bhagavad Gītā, Brahma Sūtras and Upaniṣads. As Śaṅkara interprets scripture by scripture, we also tried to interpret Śaṅkara by Śaṅkara from his authentic writings in a descriptive-analytical manner. We analyze, weight and reason the various pages in his commentaries to unearth the place he gives for *Jñāna* and *Karma* and their relationship for final release. The following conclusion is drawn:

Perhaps due to his greatness and fame, so many stories - fact and legend, historical and mythical are circulating around concerning the life and works of Śaṅkara which make it difficult for the student of religion to arrive at the factual information regarding his life, dates and place connected with him, and the works he produced. Contemporary scholars in Śaṅkara's philosophy are almost in agreement that he wrote commentaries on nine or ten principal *Upaniṣads*, *Brahma Sūtra*, *Bhagavad Gītā* and a non-commentarial treatise, *Upadeśa Sāhasrī*, but there was and is practically no settlement in regards to the facts of his life. When we study from the authentic writings of Śaṅkara, his philosophy sheds a new light; erasing the spurious interpretations we arrive at his authentic teachings – the unity of reality, the contingent reality of the world, the diverse world including human being as the name and form (*nāma rūpa*) and the extrinsic denominator or limited adjuncts (*upādhis*) of Brahman, *māyā* as the creative power of Brahman, the role of *Jñāna* and *Karma* for Self-realization and so on.

In connection with the means for salvation (liberation) our research leads us to an interesting discussion on Śaṅkara's refutation to Mīmāmsā School which emphasizes the importance of rites over against knowledge. Mīmāmsā proposes – that knowledge is part of rites, that knowledge alone does not produce liberation and that knowledge is subservient to rites. Śaṅkara successfully refuted Mīmāmsākas' stand by using various scriptural verses and said that *Jñāna* alone liberates, and that knowledge cannot be part of rites and that knowledge is not subservient to rites. However, he also pointed out the importance of rites by stating that knowledge needs the help of rites for its emergence thereby hinting the integral relationship between knowledge and works.

The research further explicates Śaṅkara's proposition that twofold Vedic religion – religion of work and religion of renunciation of work (knowledge) is ordained by God. Though these two are distinct means which cannot be conjoined, meant for two distinct classes of the people – the path of works (rites) for the ignorant and the path of knowledge for the knowledgeable (the *sannyāsins*), they are integrally related in the sense that works help people to climb the ladder of spirituality in order to attain purity of mind. Only those whose hearts are pure are eligible to tread the path of knowledge. So, these two means are complementing one another.

Śaṅkara is firmed in his commitment that knowledge alone finally serves as a mean of salvation, but does not negate the importance and obligatoriness of works because the ignorant can never achieve the saving knowledge unless they start with disintegrated work. So, *karma yoga* leads to *jñāna yoga* and *jñāna* in turns leads to Self-realization – that is but the integral relationship between *Karma Yoga* and *Jñāna Yoga* for Self-realization in Śaṅkara Advaita Vedānta.

Bibliography

I. Primary Source

Śaṅkarāchārya, *Bhagavad Gītā Bhāṣya*, translated by A. Mahadeva Shastri, Mysore: Government Oriental Library, 1901.

_______, *Brahmasūtras Bhāṣya,* translated by Swami Gambhirananda, Calcutta: Advaita Ashrama, 1993.

_______, *Upadeśasāhasrī,* translated by Swami Jagadananda, Madras: Sri Ramakrishna Math, 1989.

_______, *Bṛihadāraṇyaka Upaniṣad Bhāṣya*, translated by Swami Mahavananda; Mayavati: Advaita Ashrama, 1950.

II. Secondary Source

1. Books

Aier, T.S. Narayana, *The Age of Śaṅkara*, Madras: B.G. Paul & Co., 1971; first published in 1916.

Aleaz, K.P., *The Relevance of Relation in Śaṅkara's Advaita Vedānta*, Delhi: Kant Publications, 1996.

Chatterjee, Satischandra and Dhirendramohan Datta, *An Introduction to Indian Philosophy,* Calcutta: University of Calcutta, 2004.

Dasgupta, Surendranath, *A History of Indian Philosophy*, Vol. II, Delhi: Motilal Banarsidass, 1975 – first published in 1922 by Cambridge University Press.

Hiriyanna, M., *Outlines of Indian Philosophy*, Delhi: Motilal Banarsidass, 2000.

Krishnaswami Aiyer, C.N. "Life and Time of Śaṅkara", in *Three Great Acharyas: Śankara, Ramanuja, Madhwa: Critical Sketches of their Life and Times, an Expositions of their Philosophical System*, Madras: G.A. Natesan & Co., Publishers, n.d.

Madhva-Vidyaranya, *Śaṅkara-Dig-Vijaya: The Traditional Life of Sri Śankarācharya*, translated by Swami Tapasyananda, Madras: Sri Ramakrishna Math, N.a.

Mahadevan, T.M.P., *Śaṅkarācharya*, New Delhi: National Book Trust, India, 1968.

Marcaurelle, Roger, *Freedom through Inner Renunciation: Śaṅkara's Philosophy in a New Light*, Delhi: Sri Satguru Publications, 2002.

Prithipal, D., *Advaita Vedanta: Action and Contemplation*, Varanasi: Bharatiya Vidya Prakasan, 1969.

Tiwari, Kapil N., *Dimensions of Renunciation in Advaita Vedānta*, Delhi: Motilal Banarsidass, 1977.

Urquhart, W.S., *The Vedanta and Modern Thought*, London: Oxford University Press, 1928.

Warrier, A.G. Krishna, *The Concept of Mukti in Advaita Vedānta*, Madras: University of Madras, 1981.

2. Edited Books

Bhattacharya, Surendranath, "The Philosophy of Śaṅkara", in *The Cultural Heritage of India*, Vol. III, edited by Haridas Bhattacharyya, Calcutta: Ramakrishna Mission Institute of Culture, 1993, pp. 237-244.

Potter, Karl H., "Introduction to the Philosophy of Advaita Vedānta", in *Encyclopedia of Indian Philosophies: Advaita Vedānta up to Śaṃkara and His Pupils, Vol. III,* edited by Karl H. Potter, Delhi: Motilal Banarsidass, 1981, pp. 3-100.

Smet, R. De, "Śaṅkara's Non-dualism (Advaita-Vāda)", in *Religious Hinduism*, edited by R. De Smet and J. Neuner, Fourth Revised Edition, (Mumbai: St. Pauls, 1997), pp. 80-96.

3. Internet Source

Iyer, V. Subrahmanya, "Śaṅkara's Philosophy and Action" in *http://www.yabaluri.org/TRIVENI/CDWEB/Shankaras PhilosophyandAction1941.htm (22.11.2011).*